TRENCH WARFARE

ESSENTIAL LIBRARY OF
WORLD WAR I

Essential Library

An Imprint of Abdo Publishing
abdopublishing.com

BY SUE BRADFORD EDWARDS

CONTENT CONSULTANT

JUSTIN QUINN OLMSTEAD, PHD
ASSISTANT PROFESSOR OF HISTORY
UNIVERSITY OF CENTRAL OKLAHOMA

abdopublishing.com

Published by Abdo Publishing, a division of ABDO, PO Box 398166, Minneapolis, Minnesota 55439. Copyright © 2016 by Abdo Consulting Group, Inc. International copyrights reserved in all countries. No part of this book may be reproduced in any form without written permission from the publisher. Essential Library™ is a trademark and logo of Abdo Publishing.

Printed in the United States of America, North Mankato, Minnesota

102015
012016

Cover Photo: Everett Historical/Shutterstock Images
Interior Photos: Everett Historical/Shutterstock Images, 1, 11, 20, 25, 32, 39, 47, 56, 59, 63, 72, 88, 91; Official/Mirrorpix/Newscom, 4; AP Images, 9; akg-images/Newscom, 12, 66, 98 (top); World History Archive/Newscom, 15, 17; Bain News Service/Library of Congress, 18; Vaughan Sam/Shutterstock Images, 22; Red Line Editorial, 30–31; Hulton-Deutsch Collection/Corbis, 36; The Royal Society, 37; Sammlung Sauer/Picture-Alliance/zb/Newscom, 41; John Warwick Brooke/Imperial War Museum, 42; Agence Rol, 44; Mary Evans Picture Library/Alamy, 51, 99 (top); Contemporary Photograph, 53; Daily Mirror/Mirrorpix/Corbis, 55; Tangopaso, 65; Public Domain, 69; Emilio Segrè Visual Archives/American Institute of Physics/Science Source, 70; Shutterstock Images, 76, 93, 98 (bottom); George Mewes/Mirrorpix/Newscom, 81; Lebrecht Music & Arts/Corbis, 82; Bettmann/Corbis, 84; Corbis, 86; Mirrorpix/Newscom, 96, 99 (bottom)

Editor: Jenna Gleisner
Series Designers: Kelsey Oseid and Maggie Villaume

Library of Congress Control Number: 2015945638

Cataloging-in-Publication Data

Edwards, Sue Bradford.
 Trench warfare / Sue Bradford Edwards.
  p. cm. -- (Essential library of World War I)
ISBN 978-1-62403-924-9 (lib. bdg.)
Includes bibliographical references and index.
1. World War, 1914-1918--Trench warfare--Juvenile literature. 2. World War, 1914-1918--Campaigns--Western front-- Juvenile literature.   I. Title.
940.4/14--dc23

CONTENTS

CHAPTER 1   A PECULIAR FOG...4

CHAPTER 2   TEMPORARY TRENCHES TURNED LONG-TERM................................12

CHAPTER 3   TRENCH DESIGNS 22

CHAPTER 4   MEDICAL MATTERS.. 32

CHAPTER 5   ADAPTING TO TRENCH WARFARE 42

CHAPTER 6   DAILY SCHEDULE... 56

CHAPTER 7   CHEMICAL WARFARE 66

CHAPTER 8   TRENCHES OUTSIDE THE WESTERN FRONT 76

CHAPTER 9   LEAVING THE TRENCHES 88

Moroccan and Algerian soldiers of the French army lie dead in their trenches after exposure to the April 22, 1915, chlorine gas attack.

A PECULIAR FOG

April 22, 1915, was like most days in the trenches of the western front, the battle zone that ran from Switzerland through Belgium during World War I (1914–1918). Without the shelling of a major battle, the men went about their daily routine, each army—the Central powers and Allied forces—quietly keeping an eye on the other. Austria-Hungary, Germany, and the Ottoman Empire made up the Central powers. The United Kingdom, France, and Russia made up the Allied forces, with Japan, Italy, and the United States joining later. The Allied forces had seen very few signs of activity along the German trenches in April 1915, so the Algerian regulars who manned this section of the French defenses north of the town of Ypres, Belgium, started preparing their evening meal.

"DULCE ET DECORUM EST"

"Gas! Gas! Quick, boys! – An ecstasy of fumbling,

Fitting the clumsy helmets just in time;

But someone still was yelling out and stumbling,

And flound'ring like a man in fire or lime . . .

Dim, through the misty panes and thick green light,

As under a green sea, I saw him drowning.

In all my dreams, before my helpless sight,

He plunges at me, guttering, choking, drowning."[1]

Many soldiers used poetry to describe what they experienced throughout the war. This excerpt of "Dulce et Decorum Est," written by British soldier Wilfred Owen followed a gas attack similar to the one at Ypres. His Latin title is part of a saying from a poem that was written by the ancient Roman author Horace: *"Dulce et decorum est pro patria mori."* Translated, it means "It is sweet and right to die for your country."

It was technically spring, but the weather had been slow to warm up in Ypres. This meant the temperature quickly dropped in the late afternoon. There was only a slight breeze when the men noticed a mist forming along the German trenches. The greenish-yellow cloud seemed to rise up out of the ground. It grew taller and slowly blotted out the sunlight as it rolled toward the French line. The vapor followed the ground closely, filling shell holes and other indentations while continuing forward with the breeze.

It was like nothing these soldiers had ever seen before, and they watched it curiously. As it enveloped the first few men, the trapped soldiers choked and fought to breathe. Their fellows watched as the vapor's victims staggered out of the cloud, blinded and coughing. Their chests heaved as their lungs fought to pull in air, their faces purple with the strain.

Curiosity turned to panic. The men still didn't know what the cloud contained, but they broke ranks and ran. As they struggled to stay ahead of this mysterious threat, they abandoned their posts in the Allied trenches.

WARNING!

On April 22, 1915, Ypres became the site of the first successful chlorine gas attack in World War I. Chlorine is a chemical that, when in gas form, reacts with the water in airways and eyes to create an acid. Soldiers who were exposed to it choked as their throats and lungs swelled, and they fought to breathe, coughing and vomiting. The attack at Ypres took both the French and British commands completely by surprise, even though it was not the first chemical attack. Both the Allies and the Germans had used tear gas earlier in the war. Tear gas is a nerve gas that acts

GAS FRIGHT

The panic caused by chemical weapons was almost more damaging than the weapons themselves. Many soldiers developed what became known as gas fright, the delusion they were under gas attack. Often, several times throughout the night, someone would sound a horn or beat on an empty shell casing to sound the alarm of a gas attack. Men would scramble into their gas masks, waking their neighbors, and the panic would travel down the trench. Eventually, someone would send an all clear. Depending on the type of chemical, gas could be released from canisters or delivered in artillery shells. This meant men often suspected any explosion was a gas attack and showed symptoms, including stomachaches and vomiting, whether they had been gassed or not. As the war and gas attacks continued, it became increasingly difficult for doctors to tell who had been gassed and who had not.

against the body's pain sensors, especially in the eyes, nose, and lungs. People who are gassed cry and cough and may vomit. Military leaders had hoped tear gas would cause enough havoc in enemy trenches to allow an attacking force to sweep through and break into open countryside. When this failed, the Germans looked for a more effective agent and found it in chlorine gas.

In 1907, Germany, the United Kingdom, France, Russia, and other countries had signed the Hague Treaty, which banned certain weapons, including poisonous gases. Perhaps it was because of this agreement the Allied leaders ignored both the precedent for using chemical weapons and the warnings from intelligence something new was about to happen. The result was Allied troops had neither the protective equipment nor the training needed to face this new weapon, and because of this, the gas took a heavy toll.

THE HAGUE TREATY

In 1899 and 1907, Russia's Czar Nicholas II called the major global powers together to negotiate rules for future wars. The nations met in the Netherlands and discussed what kinds of weapons they would not produce. Among these weapons were shells or other ways to deliver poisonous or suffocating gases. Because the British had signed the treaty, they limited their researchers' attempts at the Imperial College of Science to develop a gas weapon. Germany saw poisonous gases as one way to leave the trenches, but they didn't want to be the first to break the treaty. In August 1914, the French used chemical grenades, which gave the Germans the excuse they needed to develop and use chlorine gas now that the treaty had been violated.

DEAD AND DAMAGED

It is hard to say just how many men were affected by the chlorine gas at Ypres. Many

German Red Cross workers bring liquids to those affected by chlorine gas.

SECOND PLACE

Throughout World War I, the United Kingdom and France often found themselves struggling to catch up with German technologically.

- The Germans had been the first to develop chlorine gas. The British followed suit only after encountering the deadly agent at Ypres.
- The Germans were the first to dig a line of defensive trenches, forcing the British and French to develop their own trenches in a less favorable location.
- Only after they came across a dead German pilot did the British think to develop a lightweight oxygen mask similar to the Germans'.

sources estimate there were as many as 15,000 soldiers gassed, with 5,000 killed, but the French kept no records of the numbers of casualties. Other sources, compiled from British ambulance reports and medical stations, claim there were closer to 7,000 casualties, with 350 of the men eventually dying as a result of chlorine gas exposure.[2]

Whether the total number of casualties was 15,000 or 7,000, the damage took place in approximately ten minutes. The events at Ypres showed combatants on both sides that chemical weapons could work quickly and effectively, even against soldiers sheltering in trenches.

When the French troops were hit with the gas, they panicked and broke ranks, opening up the Allied line for a stretch of no less than three miles (5 km). Wearing gas masks, the German troops left their own trenches and advanced 200 yards (180 m) into Allied territory.

Germans were prepared and protected with gas masks at the time of the Ypres chlorine gas attack.

The German plan to use chlorine gas to break through the Allied trench line worked, but only to a point. German troops, fearing the gas, advanced slowly and cautiously instead of seizing this opportunity to take the war out of the trenches and back into the open countryside where they could maneuver and win. As dusk fell, the German infantrymen sheltered in place. They had made the first advance in months but needed the light of dawn and reinforcements from headquarters to stay out of the trenches.

Left to right: Black Hand members Trifko Grabez, Nedeljko Cabrinovic, and Gavrilo Princip, in May 1914

CHAPTER

★ 2 ★

TEMPORARY TRENCHES TURNED LONG-TERM

World War I started with Serbia, a small country with nationalistic dreams. In 1835, Serbia had become independent from the Ottoman Empire, the modern country of Turkey. Soon Serbian leaders started talking about creating a country that included the majority of Serbian peoples as well as the lands they had lived on for generations. To create this country, Serbia would need to take over the neighboring country of Bosnia-Herzegovina, which had a large Serbian population.

The Serbian plan was put into jeopardy when Austria-Hungary annexed Bosnia-Herzegovina on October 6, 1908. Austria-Hungary had controlled Bosnia-Herzegovina since 1878, when it took

NATIONALISM

In the 1800s, a political idea called nationalism developed throughout Europe. Nationalism is the idea that people who share the same language and culture and have the same history should be a nation, occupying the land where they have lived for generations. The people should also govern themselves, meaning they should not be under the rule of a foreign king or czar, but instead pass their own laws and plan for their own future. Serbia wanted to unite with Bosnia-Herzegovina to create a unified Serbian nation, ruled by the Serbian people.

the region over from the Ottomans. To gain control of the Serbian peoples and lands in Bosnia-Herzegovina, Dragutin Dimitrijević, known as Colonel Apis, the head of Serbian military intelligence and a secret Serbian military group called the Black Hand, put a plan into place to weaken Austria-Hungary by killing a key political figure.

On June 28, 1914, Gavrilo Princip, a member of the Black Hand, assassinated Archduke Franz Ferdinand, the heir to the Hapsburg throne and a key leader in Austria-Hungary. It took Austria-Hungary until July 28 to declare war against Serbia. At this point, a host of alliances came into play, with Germany backing Austria-Hungary and Russia, France, and the United Kingdom supporting Serbia. With one assassination, Europe was at war, and Germany was faced with a war on two fronts.

THE SCHLIEFFEN PLAN

A war against France and the United Kingdom to the west and Russia to the east meant Germany would have to split its men and equipment into two

Gavrilo Princip, *center*, was arrested for the assassination of Archduke Franz Ferdinand.

separate, smaller forces. Many German leaders believed their nation would lose a prolonged two-front war. The only solution would be a quick, decisive victory on one front.

To this end, the Germans launched the Schlieffen Plan, which had been created by the former head of the German General Staff, Count Alfred Graf von Schlieffen, nearly a decade before the war. His strategy depended on avoiding the heavily defended French border by sweeping down through Belgium and moving through France west of Paris, France. Using this plan, German leaders believed they would quickly defeat France before Russia was ready to fight.

For this plan to work, the Germans would have to carefully coordinate the movements of their troops over a vast area. A delay in troop movements or movement to the wrong location would create a gap and make the German army vulnerable to attack by the French because Paris was a major military center. Germany invaded Belgium on August 4, 1914.

BATTLING IN BELGIUM AND FRANCE

As the Germans moved into Belgium, they immediately faced two problems. First, the Belgian army, though small, was putting up a valiant resistance because it was determined to slow the German advance as much as possible. Secondly, the Russians were gearing up for war much faster than the Germans had believed possible. Because of this, two German corps had been transferred to the eastern front, requiring the remaining forces to cover more territory than previously planned.

General Alexander von Kluck, a key German commander, didn't approach Paris until September because of the resistance posed by the Belgian and British armies. Believing he no longer had the manpower to go west of the city, von Kluck led his men to the east of Paris. This meant he was deviating from the Schlieffen Plan and, because his men were not where they were expected to be, he left a gap in the German line. This new route exposed von Kluck's flank to the French, who saw their opportunity and attacked.

The battle of the Marne was crucial for both sides. If the Germans pushed forward and took Paris, the western front would be lost to the Allies. If the Allies

The German cavalry invaded Spa, Belgium, on August 4, 1914.

ALEXANDER VON KLUCK

1846–1934

Alexander von Kluck was a soldier's soldier, spending his military career fighting alongside troops instead of manning a command center. When World War I started, this aggressive commander was given charge of the German First Army.

Von Kluck was ordered to send his army west of Paris, a path that would leave him and his men badly isolated from the rest of the German forces; this had been a problem with the plan from the start. Because he felt he did not have the manpower to complete the maneuver, von Kluck led his men to the east of Paris, opening up a gap in the German line. Because of this, von Kluck is often blamed for the failure of the Schlieffen Plan and was mocked in a popular British marching song sung to the tune of "Pop Goes the Weasel."

Throughout the war, von Kluck wrote a memoir titled *The March on Paris*. In it, von Kluck kept descriptions to a minimum and seldom spoke of how he felt about what was happening. Instead, he reported on events as they took place. Von Kluck was wounded in the leg in March 1915. He retired from service in October 1916.

forced the Germans back, they would split the German army in two. To avoid this, von Kluck was given the order to retreat.

DIGGING IN

The German retreat was a carefully planned withdrawal. The Germans had taken the time to locate a solid defensive position on high ground above the River Aisne. Along this ridge, they had excavated trenches to shelter their men as they took a stand and fought to halt the Allied advance. In the Chinese classic Sun Tzu's *Art of War*, which was written nearly 2,500 years ago, military leaders are advised not to attack an enemy that is positioned on high ground because this enemy can easily mount an ambush. The Germans used this strategy when they took up a position in their trenches above the Aisne.

FLANKS

The most vulnerable part of any army on the move is the flank, or the extreme ends or sides of the group of men. As an army moves forward, the center drives the enemy before the main body of this military force. The flank is in danger of passing the enemy and having its back to enemy soldiers. If this happens, the soldiers in the flank cannot fire on the enemy without turning, which can be difficult to do in the heat of battle. In the Schlieffen Plan, von Kluck was to pass Paris, which meant exposing his flank to enemy forces.

From the trenches, the Germans could shoot at approaching Allied troops to keep them back. The Allied forces' best strategy to get the Germans out of

French soldiers await a German assault during the battle of the Marne.

a set of trenches was to fire on them from a distance using heavy artillery. Unfortunately, the Allies didn't have enough massive guns to do the job. Because of this, the Allies built their own trenches below the German fortifications. These trenches would provide their men with necessary shelter as they struggled to force the Germans back.

The Allies planned to do this by extending their own trenches out far enough north so they could outflank the Germans and fire on them from behind. The Germans extended their trenches northward as well, struggling to outflank the Allies. Neither side succeeded, but the push northward became known as the Race to the Sea, stopping only when both sides reached the North Sea. At this point, two sets of trenches stretched from Switzerland to the English Channel, a total of 440 miles (700 km). No longer a quick fix, the trenches along the western front became a long-term battle strategy.

DIVIDED POWER IN ALLIED TRENCHES

Control and responsibility for the Allied Trenches was divided among various Allied armies. The Belgian army and forces of the United Kingdom manned Allied trenches in Northern France and Belgium. These forces included troops from the British Isles as well as their colonies, overseas nations that were ruled by the king of the United Kingdom. The rest of the Allied trenches were in the hands of French and French colonial troops, such as the Algerians. Standing against these forces were the German trenches manned by the German military.

Trenches were constructed in zigzag patterns.

TRENCH DESIGNS

In World War I, trench warfare didn't take place between one long German trench and one long Allied trench. Instead, an elaborate network of trenches provided lifesaving shelter to the soldiers on both sides of the conflict.

Each trench was a zigzag, running straight, then making a sharp bend, then running straight again, then making another bend, and so on. The reason for the zigzags was simple: in a long, straight trench, an exploding shell would collapse much more of the trench than in a zigzag trench. In addition, a single enemy soldier could drop into a straight trench and shoot men for a great distance. The corners and turns of a zigzag trench meant a bullet could only fly so far before embedding itself in a wall. This twisted configuration offered additional protection to the soldiers sheltering there.

THREE LINES OF TRENCH DEFENSE

Each trench system contained three parallel trenches and the trenches connecting them. The trench nearest the enemy, called the firing trench or firing line, was the first line of defense and the point from which a group of soldiers watched and fired on the enemy. The second trench lay 200 to 500 yards (180 to 460 m) behind the firing trench. This support trench provided a second line of defense. If the enemy managed to capture the firing trench, soldiers could retreat to the support trench. Several hundred yards behind the support trench lay the reserve trench. In this trench, men waited to take their places in the more stressful firing trench. In addition to being something of a waiting room, this last trench provided a place to store the supplies an army might need at short notice.

Connecting these three parallel trenches were the communication trenches. Again, no single communication trench provided a straight passage from

TRENCH SIGNS

The interconnected system of zigzagging trenches was a confusing place and was hard for stressed soldiers to navigate. A soldier could easily get turned around and think he was farther down the trench line than he really was. To avoid this confusion, the men posted signs. Some of the signs pointed toward various places on the front line. Others marked important points in the trench systems themselves. Soldiers gave important spots names from home, such as Piccadilly Circus, a well-known square in the center of London, or Hyde Park Corner, an intersection beside one of London's royal parks.

Serbian soldiers watch and take aim from a firing trench.

the firing trench to the reserve trench. One communication trench ran between the firing trench and the support trench, and, to one side of this communication trench, another ran from the support trench to the reserve trench. In addition to providing sheltered passage from trench to trench, communication trenches housed the dugouts and dressing stations that provided additional shelter for the men and a place to dress wounds.

Because the trenches had to be deep enough to protect the men from enemy fire, sandbags were stacked atop the walls in areas where the soil was too shallow to dig a deeper trench. Although all of the trenches had a reputation for being wet, dirty, and miserable, the Allied trenches were much worse than German trenches in these respects.

DUGOUTS

Dugouts, or rooms dug off the side of a trench, provided soldiers with shelter from weather but also from enemy artillery fire. Men in the firing line could spend their time in the dugouts when not on duty. These shelters were places for sleeping or emergency first aid, depending on the size and the construction. The smallest, which were called funk holes, were only large enough to shelter two sleeping men. Wooden posts and metal supported larger dugouts, and some had plank walls. Deep dugouts were ten feet (3 m) deep and accessible by stairs.

GERMANS NOT JUST BETTER BUILDERS

Some people believe the German trenches were dryer and more comfortable than the Allied trenches because the Germans were better builders. It is true only some of the Allied trenches had slatted duckboard lining the floors, and everywhere else, the men stood in ankle-deep water. But Allied trenches weren't wetter just because Germans may have been better builders. The Germans had carefully located their trenches along high ground for defensive purposes. As luck would have it, these hilltop locations meant their trenches lay above the water table. Naturally occurring groundwater, found in cracks and spaces in soil and rock, wasn't prone to seep in from the bottom. Along the Vimy Ridge in northern France, German trenches were dug into chalk limestone. Near Ypres, German trenches ran through clayey sand. Both types of soil drain well, so even when it rained, the water would seep back out of the German trenches.

The Allies, on the other hand, realized they needed trenches only after the Germans had taken shelter in their own carefully constructed earthworks. This meant Allied trenches were positioned in relation to the German trenches. Because the Germans had chosen the hilltops, the Allies built in the lowlands facing the German trenches. These lowland

SANDLESS SANDBAGS

Because Allied trenches were often dug where the water table was high, the men could dig down only so far before hitting water. To make the trenches deep enough, they added height to the tops of the trenches with sandbags. Because they didn't have access to sand to fill these cloth bags, they filled the bags with dirt. A bag three-quarters full weighed approximately 60 pounds (27 kg). In addition to being used to build up the walls, the bags were also stacked around the men's feet and legs at night in an attempt to keep warm.

BRACING THE TRENCHES

The Allies had to brace their trenches because of lateral pressure, or sideways pressure, from water in the soil. This water pressure was a problem because the Allies had to dig their trenches in low-lying areas where the groundwater is near the surface. The Germans had to brace their trenches as well, but for a different reason. German trenches were dug in sandy clays that tended to shift, causing walls to crumble.

trenches were much closer to the water table and, if they dug too far down, water would seep into the trenches. Even when Allied trenches were in soil that drained well, the topsoil was often so shallow the base of the trench sat atop a layer of clay. Clay drains so slowly that if a trench filled with a foot of water, it took three dry days for the water to drain. Despite these wet conditions, the trenches provided shelter, which no-man's-land did not.

NO-MAN'S-LAND

Between the German and Allied trenches lay an unclaimed strip known as no-man's-land. In some areas, it was hundreds of yards wide. In others, it was so narrow that each side, hidden in their trenches, could hear enemy soldiers talking. Soldiers had to cross this strip of earth to attack the enemy, but it was all but impossible to make it across. Crossing soldiers faced constant bombardment by heavy artillery and machine gun placements positioned to guarantee interlacing fire across the entire area.

Periods of rain accompanied by artillery bombardment meant the water and soil were churned together by the explosions, creating a muddy wasteland. In Ypres, the mud was so deep a man could drown. Shell holes also marked the landscape. Some of them were as deep as a man was tall. If one of these craters filled with water, a soldier might duck to avoid a shell or slip while carrying a heavy pack and slide down into the water and drown.

Narrow or wide, no-man's-land stretched out like a scarred lunar landscape. Wilfred Owen, a soldier and poet from the United Kingdom explained, "No-man's-land under snow is like the face of the moon: chaotic, crater ridden, uninhabitable, awful, the abode of madness."[1]

TRENCH DESIGN

NO-MAN'S-LAND

DRESSING STATION

COMMUNICATION TRENCHES

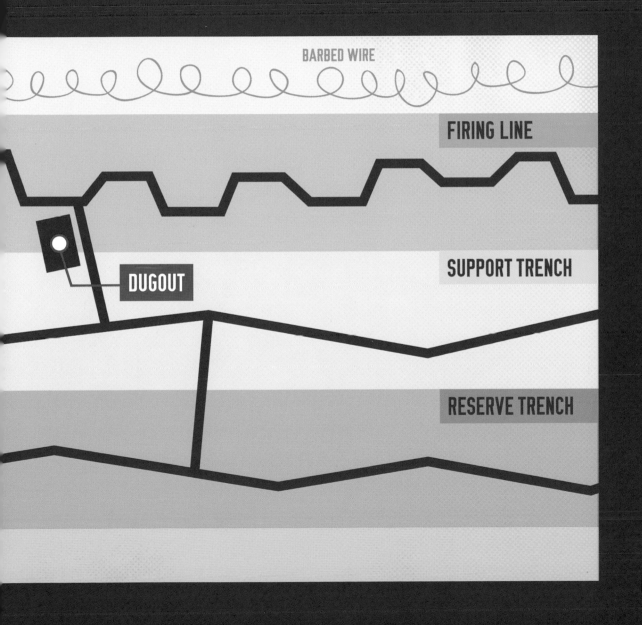

BARBED WIRE

FIRING LINE

SUPPORT TRENCH

DUGOUT

RESERVE TRENCH

Life in the trenches was anything but pleasant as soldiers faced harsh and uncomfortable conditions in addition to the fears of war.

MEDICAL MATTERS

While the trenches provided soldiers with lifesaving shelter, the time spent there was also an assault on the senses. Temperatures ranged from summer's heat to winter's freezing cold. Decomposing bodies and latrines created an appalling stench. The pounding sound of artillery fire was so relentless it led to a form of mental illness unseen in earlier wars.

SHELL SHOCK

Doctors today talk about post-traumatic stress disorder (PTSD), a mental health condition caused when someone, such as a soldier, is traumatized physically or mentally by the events happening to or around him or her. Symptoms include anxiety, nightmares, and

TOILET TROUBLES

Latrine trenches and pits were generally located out of sight of the enemy but near the trenches that sheltered the men. Smaller pit latrines were sometimes located in a dead end in the main trench system. Regardless of where the latrines were, men relieved themselves as quickly as possible, because the smell of an open latrine used by large numbers of men for days on end was extraordinary. Lye, a caustic chemical that eats away at flesh and waste, was used to reduce the amount of waste and thus the smell, but the smell was so bad men often relieved themselves in cookie tins they could dump outside the trench.

flashbacks, in which the traumatic events are replayed in the sufferer's mind.

In World War I, commanding officers saw similar symptoms. At first, some officers thought their men were acting cowardly in an attempt to avoid battle, but they slowly realized something was truly wrong with these men's minds. They determined the source of the symptoms was the loud noises, physical shock, and stress of long-term heavy shelling. Some people called it shell shock. Other times, it was called nerves, because of the edgy, nervous way the men behaved.

The military wanted these men cured so they could return to the front line to fight, but shell shock wasn't something that could be treated in a nearby dressing station close to the shelling. Dressing stations dealt with gunshots and broken bones, applying splints and stopping bleeding. Men with shell shock were sent to hospitals in their home countries, where their sheer numbers created problems as doctors tried to find enough space for all the patients. The fighting in Ypres alone sent 600 soldiers back to New Zealand for rest, recovery, and treatment.[1]

Treatments for shell shock varied from doctor to doctor but most often included rest, hot meals, and exercise, including forced marches. Major Dudley Carmalt-Jones, in charge of a facility outside of Ypres, used hot-water bottles for pain but also treated patients who seemed especially dazed with electric shock, passing electric currents through the brain to cause a seizure. In contrast, Captain William Rivers is still famous for developing a conversation-based therapy he called the talking cure.

DRESSING STATIONS

Because dressing stations provided emergency first aid, they were located near the front line. In mobile combat, this might be an existing building, but in trench warfare this often meant a dugout. The dressing stations were manned by ambulance crews or members of the Red Cross, an international group that cares for the wounded and sick. Men with minor injuries were cleaned up, bandaged, and returned to duty. More seriously injured men were prepared for transportation to a clearing station. These preparations might include splinting a bone, stopping bleeding, or even amputating a limb. From the clearing station, soldiers with serious injuries or those who were gravely ill could be transported to a hospital away from the fighting.

TRENCH FOOT

In addition to shelling, the men faced the dangers of heavy rain. Constant rainfall meant soldiers wearing tight boots stood in ankle-deep water, where they were in danger of contracting a fungal infection known as trench foot. The first symptoms of trench foot were blistering and swelling, with the foot sometimes reaching two or three times its normal size. Often the man would lose the feeling in his swollen feet, but a lack of pain was

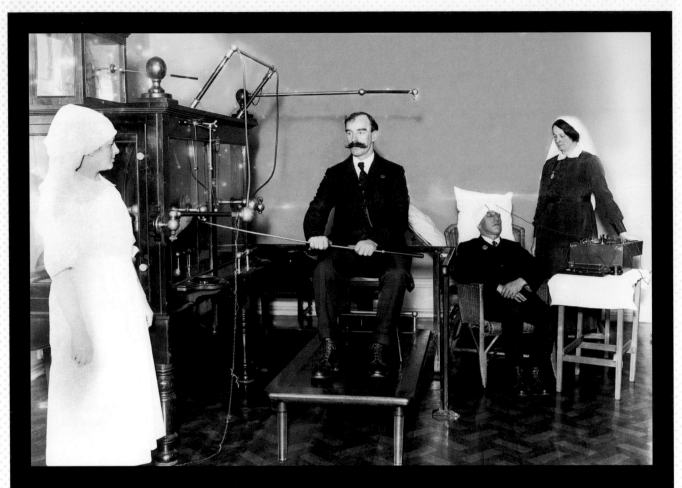

Soldiers receive electric shock therapy in 1915.

not good news. Lack of blood flow to the infected area could lead to gangrene, a condition in which skin and muscle die and the foot or leg must be amputated.

To prevent trench foot, the men were ordered to put on dry socks and boots as often as possible and to use a protective coating, such as whale oil, on their

CAPTAIN WILLIAM RIVERS

1864–1922

William Halse Rivers was born in Kent, England, in 1864. He attended the University of London and graduated with a degree in medicine in 1886 when he was only 22 years old. Before working with shell-shock victims in World War I, Rivers took part in an anthropological expedition to the Torres Straits in Australia in 1898. There, he studied kinship among the people of the Solomon Islands. He was among the early anthropologists who lived for a time among the people he studied, a practice now called participant observation.

In his work with shell-shock patients at Craiglockhart War Hospital in Scotland, he developed what is known as the talking cure. Using this method, Rivers interacted with his patients and encouraged them to confront their fears and the horrors they had witnessed by discussing them. This went against the soldiers' commanding officers and even their families' expectations of them, which most often demanded the men be silent and brave. Rivers was hired to cure his patients of shell shock so they could return to the fighting, but he believed sending the soldiers back put the men in grave danger of again developing shell shock; despite this, Rivers' superiors continued to return patients to duty as soon as they were able to function.

THOMAS SPLINT

Surgeon Hugh Owen Thomas invented the Thomas splint in the late 1800s to keep people with broken femurs from bleeding to death. His nephew, Sir Robert Jones, a major general inspector for orthopedics, first used this lifesaving device in battlefield medicine. With the Thomas splint, a wire ring fits around the patient's upper thigh, while a U-shaped piece of heavy wire extends the length of the leg. The leg can be bandaged to the splint, straightening and supporting the broken bone and keeping it from cutting blood vessels and muscle. Broken femurs, the long bone of the thigh, generally cause extensive bleeding if not properly stabilized. When World War I began in 1914, 80 percent of soldiers who had this injury died. By 1916, with the use of the Thomas splint, 80 percent of soldiers with this injury survived.[3]

feet. They often did stamping drills to get their blood flowing and warm up cold, unused muscles. Officers also inspected their men's feet daily, looking for swelling or blistering.

CREEPY CRAWLIES

As if the stresses of shelling and the fear of trench foot weren't enough, the men in the trenches had to share their space with both lice and rats. Two kinds of rats, black and brown, came into the trenches in search of food scraps. The rodents also ventured out into no-man's-land, dining on the corpses of downed soldiers, always starting with the eyes. Even more disturbing was that the rats didn't always wait for an injured man to die: "On the fire step in the trenches during the night, you could hear the groaning of the dying—but you couldn't go out to help them. There were rats feeding on their flesh," said British private Cecil Withers.[2]

Sometimes, when a man lay down to sleep, a rat would run across his face. In addition to feeding on corpses and food scraps, the rats sometimes got into the men's stored provisions and ruined their food supplies. There was also a fear rats and the fleas they carried might carry disease.

The men had orders not to shoot these hated rats because it wasted ammunition, but sometimes a disgusted soldier would take a shot. Soldiers also bayoneted the rats and clubbed them, but with the constant food supply provided by fallen friends and foe, the numbers of rats grew, reaching the millions.

Trench foot was an almost constant threat as Allied soldiers were exposed to wet conditions and did not often have clean, dry socks to change into.

Although not as visible as the rats, lice were just as common and lived on the men themselves. Lice bred in the seams of the men's uniforms and, as the men huddled together for warmth, moved from one man to another. Only in the last year of the war did doctors realize lice spread an illness known as trench fever, which included a high fever followed by severe pain. When one of the tiny parasites bit a sick man and then bit a healthy man, the fever spread from one man to another. Trench fever wasn't life threatening, but approximately 15 percent of the trench-bound soldiers caught it and required up to 12 weeks out of the trenches to recover.[4] There was no vaccine to ward off trench fever.

VACCINES

With so many men in constant contact, vaccinations became incredibly important for slowing the spread of disease. In 1909, US doctors had created a vaccine for typhoid, a fever caused by the salmonella bacteria. The vaccine was prepared at the Army Medical School and administered to soldiers. It was so effective that although there were 20,000 documented cases of typhoid during the Spanish-American War in 1898, there were only 1,500 cases in World War I.[5]

Even before the men knew lice spread trench fever, they hated the itchy red bumps that sprang up wherever the tiny insects bit. The men gathered in groups to delouse, picking insects off each other and running the flame of a candle down the seams of their clothing so the heat would kill the lice gathered there. Soldiers also periodically dunked clothing in a Naphthalene solution. This oil-based chemical was used to ward off insects, including lice and cloth-eating moths.

Although these attempts could kill or drive away adult lice, the eggs were never all destroyed, and a few hours after a man put his clothing back on, his body heat would cause the eggs to hatch. Lice, rats, infection, and wet conditions added to the stench and misery of the trenches.

Delousing was a common activity in the trenches.

Soldiers got used to sleeping, eating, and living in the trenches.

ADAPTING TO TRENCH WARFARE

Before World War I, traditional warfare involved armies moving across fields and through forests. Cavalry traveled swiftly on horseback, draft animals hauled cannons, and foot soldiers marched to the field of combat. The trenches of World War I tied everyone and everything down. Trench warfare dramatically changed the nature of the fighting, so much so that once the men reached the trenches, much of the training they had already received became irrelevant. They had to relearn even the most basic war tactics, including checking their enemy's position.

Down in the trenches, the soldiers could be safe, but they couldn't see what the enemy was doing. If a soldier stood on the

fire step and peeked up over the rim, he was likely to get shot by snipers who watched for men to peer out of the trench.

To give entrenched soldiers a view of their enemy, the militaries of both sides developed periscopes similar to the larger viewers later used on submarines. Using a handheld periscope, a soldier could see a mirror's reflection of what the enemy was doing without putting his head up where the enemy would see him. Specially rigged rifles also allowed soldiers to peer over the top and use a mechanism to fire the rifle, all from the shelter of the trenches.

Between sniper fire and the shrapnel from artillery shells, World War I saw so many head injuries that even the men's basic equipment needed updating.

French soldiers peer through a periscope at the enemy.

By 1915, the French were giving their soldiers steel helmets. The British also started distributing helmets, and the Germans, who already used helmets, switched from the distinctive *Pickelhaube* design, with its easy-to-spot spike, to the steel coal-scuttle style, with a rounded helmet flaring out slightly over the ears and neck, worn into World War II (1939–1945). Helmets and periscopes made it into the trenches, where they helped keep men safe. But many proposed weapons never made it past the idea stage. Others, such as barbed wire, found new uses in the war.

WACKY WEAPONS

These wacky weapons never made it off of the drawing board and into combat:

- A huge pump that spewed streams of concrete through a hose and into the German trenches
- Artillery shells that contained writhing masses of snakes instead of explosives or chemicals
- Magnet-toting balloons that drifted over enemy trenches, lifting rifles and machine guns into the air
- A gun with a mercury circuit that would create a light beam along which to aim; to work, it had to be kept level for the mercury to flow into place, complete the electric circuit, and ignite the light.

THORNY PROBLEMS

Barbed wire itself wasn't an entirely new idea. Before the war, US farmers had used it to fence in cattle. In World War I, barbed wire was laid down through no-man's-land, where it was fixed into place between the trenches. At first, the wire was hung from posts that had to be hammered into the ground, but hammering, even in the cover of darkness, was noisy and gave the men away.

Entanglements of wire were later hung on screw pickets, with corkscrew-shaped bases that could be quietly twisted into the ground.

While artillery could breach fortress walls and destroy machine guns, the wire proved highly resilient to blasts. Shrapnel shells fired from artillery wreaked havoc on the men, but didn't usually damage the barbed wire. A soldier with wire cutters could snip through one section, but a man attempting to crawl through this small opening became an easy, slow-moving target. If the soldier tried hurrying through the opening, he might end up hanging scarecrow-like from the wire when his clothing snagged, pinning him in place where he became an easy target. At the battle of the Somme, the Scottish men fighting in their kilts had the greatest difficulty getting through this grasping barrier, especially through narrow gaps or where the wire had not been destroyed as planned. But relatively little time was spent in major battles. Most days were spent waiting in the trenches.

FIRST BARBED WIRE

In 1874, Joseph Glidden, an Illinois cattleman, invented the first barbed wire. He wound together two strands of wire and attached the two strands together at regular intervals with a short twist of pointed wire. Before his invention, cattle would simply lean on a wire fence until they shoved it down, but the barbs on Glidden's wire kept the fences up and the cattle safely penned in.

Barbed wire proved a successful barrier between opposing troops.

LIVE AND LET LIVE

The longer both sides remained entrenched, building extensive dugouts and pillboxes, the more permanent and stationary the situation felt. This promoted a phenomenon known as "live and let live," in which soldiers went through their daily routine with no particular consideration given to confronting the enemy. In an extreme example in the Ottoman Empire at Gallipoli, the two sides bogged down within days on April 1915, and the men tossed gifts, including food and cigarettes, to each other and hung their laundry to dry on the barbed wire strung between the trenches.

The degree to which this relaxed attitude developed depended in part on which groups manned the trenches. Even the famed Christmas Truce of 1914 only encompassed small sections of the western front. Germany's Prussians were aggressive fighters, but the Bavarians, for example, were happy to let things slide. Officers feared this lackadaisical attitude, knowing relaxed men could

OBSERVATION TREES

During World War I, both sides developed schemes to spy on and secretly attack the enemy. British soldiers manned observation posts camouflaged to resemble dead trees. Craftsmen made models of blasted tree trunks and lined them with armor. Under the cover of darkness, the men would sneak the tree out of the trenches and replace a real blasted tree with their fake. An artillery spotter with a telephone would hide inside this tree and spy on the movements of Germany's big guns and troops.

easily miss an approaching enemy force. To keep the soldiers on their toes, officers planned nighttime raids.

RAIDING THE ENEMY

Nighttime raids helped keep men alert, but they also required careful planning and attention to detail. First, the soldiers swapped their bayonet-tipped rifles for spiked clubs and knives they could use in the narrow trenches. They also had to be sure to bring hand grenades. The men had to carry this gear without their packs. Raiders had to move fast, and a heavy backpack, even one full of lifesaving ammo, slowed them down and could easily hang on curls of barbed wire.

As they lined up to leave their trench and the lead soldier cut the barbed wire, the other men kept their eyes on the sky. Raids took place on moonless nights; a cloud drifting aside could expose the moon, which would then spotlight an advancing party of raiders to enemy machine gunners. Once the raiders reached the enemy trench, they tossed hand grenades into the dugouts. It was essential to keep track of how many grenades had been thrown to avoid advancing before all of the grenades had exploded.

As important as it was to keep fighters alert and focused, raids didn't take place only for this purpose. Raiders also hoped to capture prisoners who could reveal planned troop movements, adding to any information spies had gathered.

THE CHRISTMAS TRUCE

On Christmas Day, December 25, 1914, in several places along the western front, the soldiers quit firing artillery and rifles and launched an impromptu holiday celebration. Some stories say it started on Christmas Eve when men on both sides caroled, singing long and loud for both their fellows and the enemy to hear. Some German soldiers played brass instruments to accompany their carols.

At dawn, some of the German soldiers left their trenches and approached the Allied trenches, calling out "Merry Christmas." The Allies thought it was a trap until they saw the Germans were unarmed. The Allies also emerged, and soon the men were exchanging gifts of cake-like puddings and cigarettes. They took photos with enemy soldiers. There was more singing, and there were even impromptu soccer games.

Sadly, it wasn't only a time of celebration. Soldiers also took the time to retrieve the bodies of dead friends from no-man's-land for burial. Brief truces for just this purpose occurred several times early in the war but were soon halted by superior officers who worried their men weren't taking the fighting seriously enough.

A holiday truce only happened one time, and it didn't include the entire western front; for most of the front, the war continued on as usual. Although the men discussed having Christmas truces later in the war, their officers made it clear that anyone participating would be disciplined. Historians disagree about just how widespread the Christmas Truce was, but some estimates state 100,000 soldiers took part.[1] Regardless, it remains one of the most inspirational stories to come out of the war.

During the Christmas Truce of 1914, British and German soldiers shared gifts and songs.

MOLE MEN

Trenches weren't World War I's only passages through the earth. Just as important were the tunnels used to defeat trenches. Both the Allies and the Germans dug tunnels to place mines, disc-shaped bombs set off underground, beneath the enemy's trenches. Mines had first been used in the US Civil War (1861–1865), but the mines of World War I were bigger and did more damage than any mines used before.

The men who dug the trenches across no-man's-land and planted the mines were officially called tunnelers, but they referred to themselves as moles. John Norton-Griffiths, the engineer charged with developing the Royal Engineer tunneling companies, recruited these men for the British. In peacetimes, many of these men labored as miners, and they knew how to work underground, silently and swiftly excavating narrow tunnels. They had one of the most dangerous jobs of the war, in part because they could use up all of the oxygen in the tunnel and suffocate.

Poor air wasn't the only danger the moles faced. Mishandled explosives could detonate long before they reached the end of the tunnel. In addition, moles who made too much noise might attract the attention of the enemy, who would then dig through into their tunnel and engage in vicious hand-to-hand combat, fighting for their lives. At the battle of Messines at 3:10 a.m. on June 7,

JOHN NORTON-GRIFFITHS

1871–1930

John Norton-Griffiths was born on July 13, 1871. He was the head of a company excavating tunnels as part of a drainage system in Manchester, England, when the United Kingdom entered the war.

The Germans first used mines in November 1914 against the French and then again in December against the United Kingdom. When the United Kingdom tried to lay its own explosives, its men found the wet, sandy Flanders clay impossible to work because water quickly filled the tunnel. Norton-Griffiths knew his men working on the Manchester drainage tunnels could dig through the Somme soil more quickly and quietly than the Germans. He recruited men and boys who had been working the mines of the United Kingdom since they were children.

The day they arrived at the western front, they started digging using a method called clay kicking, in which one man lies on a wooden support while silently pressing a shovel-like kicking iron into the soil. He pushed the shovel blade through the soil with his feet. Removing a slab of soil, he passed it over his head to the bagger, who gathered the soil for another man to carry out of the tunnel. These men dug beneath the German trenches at Messines and continued their work as long as the fighting remained in the trenches.

WORKING MODEL

Much of the credit for devastating the German trenches at Messines goes to Field Marshal Herbert Plumer and a model of the surrounding area he made. He was known for the extraordinary amount of training his men received before a major battle; this training often included time spent with a battlefield terrain model constructed out of soil. Using this model, his men could see where to find cover, where enemies might be located, and how to maneuver through the smoke and chaos of a battle. Plumer had fought in the area of Messines early in the war and believed the region would be critical, so he trained his troops using a model, a detailed miniature that helped them picture the real thing, leading to a rousing success that showed how good planning paid off.

1917, the Allies detonated 400 short tons (363 metric tons) of mines in the tunnels beneath the German lines. After the battle, 10,000 German soldiers were listed as missing, and experts believe many of them were killed in the explosion.[2]

The Allies' blasts destroyed trenches and claimed thousands of German lives at the battle of Messines.

Soldiers on both sides were drilled to observe enemy lines and be ready for attack at any time.

DAILY SCHEDULE

Although death could come at any time in the form of a well-aimed shot, soldiers were not just sitting around waiting for this to happen. They had to be ready for an enemy attack even if that attack might be weeks away. To keep prepared, the military kept the men on a daily routine of tasks and infrequent periods of rest.

DAY-TO-DAY

Both the Germans and the Allies believed the majority of enemy attacks occurred at or near dawn. This meant every soldier's day began at some point between midnight and 4:00 a.m., when they woke up and stood to arms. Each soldier would prepare his rifle, which included attaching the bayonet, and would then mount the fire step and wait. Ironically, both the Germans and Allies did this at the same time every day, so an attack was not likely to occur with both sides watching and waiting for the other side to attack.

Next in the daily routine came a period known as the morning hate. As the sun rose, sometime between 4:00 and 6:00 a.m., a mist cloaked no-man's-land and hid any approaching enemy. Just in case an unseen enemy was coming, soldiers on both sides fired their rifles and machine guns and also some light artillery toward the enemy lines.

Because their weapons had just been fired, from 6:00 until 9:00 a.m. the soldiers cleaned their rifles, which were then inspected by their officers. Given the dirty, wet conditions of the trenches, this routine was essential to ensure guns were dirt- and rust-free and fired reliably when needed.

Once the men had seen to their personal weapons, they had approximately ten hours to fill. Some of them stood sentry duty, keeping an eye on the enemy, while others worked on trench maintenance, refilling sandbags, repairing

QUIET TIME ACTIVITIES

The horrors of battle and the dullness of the day-to-day routine left soldiers in a state of uneasy boredom. They relieved their boredom with a variety of activities, including:

- Writing: Many soldiers wrote letters home, but they also wrote poetry and kept journals.
- Games: In the trenches, many troops played card games. Behind the trenches, soldiers from the United Kingdom played soccer, which they called football.
- Souvenirs: Many men spent time seeking keepsakes. A favorite for the Allies was the German *Pickelhaube*, or spiked helmet.
- Music: Some French soldiers formed trench orchestras, making their own instruments from scrap materials.

German soldiers read and write during some idle time in the trenches.

and replacing the duckboard, and seeing to trench drainage. The men who weren't scheduled for these jobs had free time to catch up on their sleep, write letters home, or participate in whatever other hobbies they found to occupy themselves. Because the officers on both sides believed another likely time of day for an attack was at dusk, there was also an evening stand to arms sometime between 7:30 and 9:00 p.m. Again, both sides gathered at their fire steps to watch and wait.

Once night fell, the men could move around with less chance of being observed by the enemy under the cover of darkness. Between 9:00 p.m. and midnight, while some men stood watch, others fetched rations. This was also the time when men in the firing trench relocated to the reserve trench or the support trench, as well as when groups of men might be sent into no-man's-land if it was a moonless night.

LETTERS HOME

Letters from loved ones back home gave soldiers the support they needed to get through the war. When soldiers wrote home, they rarely described the realities of battle. They edited the harsher realities, sparing their loved ones the knowledge of what they themselves were experiencing. Some men filled their letters home with comforting domestic details, discussing what they had eaten for breakfast that day. Others spoke of the distraction of having so many men reliant on them they didn't have time to consider their own discomfort or worries, instead of writing about the friends killed that day. Each letter home was a battle in itself as the soldier decided whether to relieve tension by being honest or maintain a stiff upper lip. In addition, revealing too much information would lead to the letter being censored by a superior officer or postal worker who would black out or cut out sensitive information.

AWAY TIME

Between being shelled or gassed or fearing that one or the other would occur, the men experienced so much stress that both armies limited the amount of time individual men spent in the firing trenches. For the battalions from the United Kingdom, this meant they usually only spent five days a month on the front line in the firing trench. Fifteen or so days each month were spent in the reserve and support trenches, which were still stressful because of shelling and the possibility of moving back to the firing trench if there was a battle.

This left almost half of a soldier's time each month away from the trenches. The officers saw to it the men got this time in an attempt to keep them sharp and mentally able to fight. When they weren't in the trenches and had been in the military long enough, they might get to go home on leave. Those men who didn't get to go home stayed near the front and trained.

TRENCH NEWSPAPER

When a group of British soldiers found an abandoned printing press in Ypres in 1916, they decided to publish a newspaper. Because they called the Belgian town of Ypres (pronounced *Eee-prah*) *Wipers*, they named the paper the *Wipers Times*. Under Lieutenant Colonel Fred Roberts, the paper published humorous advertisements and articles that made light of the war and the situations the soldiers faced on a daily basis. One advertisement sought to sell Hill 60, an area that had been bombed into a crater, and described the hill as bright and breezy, an excellent destination for a day trip with a great view of the historic town of Ypres. Another article advised soldiers on how to cure themselves of optimism.

A lot of training involved physical exercise to keep the men in the best possible shape. Some of the men were farm boys or miners, well-muscled from doing hard physical labor, but as the war went on, men who were not as physically fit were drafted into the military. Although other European powers used the draft earlier in the war, the United Kingdom didn't do so until 1916. During a draft, the government keeps a list of men who can fight and calls up groups of men as needed. As the war dragged on, more and more of the soldiers were men who had not willingly signed up for the war, including men who had worked as clerks in shops or other labor-light jobs. The government also accepted married men, older men, and men who might have health problems. The men had to be worked and worked hard to keep them ready for when the war left the trenches.

GETTING THE MAIL

Letters from home kept up the morale of the soldiers, and letters from the sons and husbands at war also kept up the morale of family back home. But transporting and delivering the letters was not an easy task. For example, delivering mail to the trenches from the United Kingdom was an immense job:

- 2: Days it took for a letter to reach the front
- 12,500,000: Letters that left the United Kingdom for the western front each week
- 375,000: Letters censored per day. Often a soldier's superior would read a letter to make certain no military secrets had been revealed.
- 19,000: Mailbags that crossed the English Channel each day
- 134: Mail ships sunk by the enemy
- 55,000: Mailbags sent to France for the Christmas of 1917. This equated to 6,000 truckloads of mail.[1]

The United States would join the war in April 1917 and instate a draft just one month later.

TRENCH ART

Soldiers had a lot of free time on their hands, and many of them occupied themselves by creating a type of art now known as trench art. This artwork was made from materials the men salvaged from the battlefield itself: brass shell casings became vases or tobacco jars; copper driving-bands, designed to make a shell fit securely in the barrel of a gun, were turned into paper knives to open envelopes or slit uncut book pages; and pieces of wooden propellers were carved into picture frames and small boxes. Although trench art could take many different forms, many of the men reworked metal.

Metalworking was not a quiet activity the men could do in the front trenches. Because the noise of cutting, etching, and filing might draw the attention of enemy snipers, this was something soldiers did in the reserve trenches or when away from the trenches altogether. The simplest pieces were engraved with designs including flowers, faces, or the symbol of a soldier's unit or country. At first, the soldiers incised these designs with whatever they could use as a tool—a piece of a bed spring, an ice pick, or a screwdriver. Later in the war, men actually sold sets of tools and patterns other soldiers could use to make the most popular designs.

Many of the finished pieces of metalwork took more than etching to complete. Some required welding, using a flame to cut and rejoin the metal. Although soldiers enjoyed making their own pieces, sometimes men worked together; a skilled welder would do the cutting and joining while another man would prep the metal or polish the final piece.

The battle scrap used by the soldiers wasn't considered waste material by the armed forces; the military wanted as much of these materials recovered as possible to be manufactured into new weapons. Despite this, most commanding officers turned a blind eye to what their men claimed because they preferred having the soldiers busy doing something constructive instead of sitting around with idle hands and worried minds.

Two shell cases engraved with "Hurlus" and "Tahure," two villages in Marne

Chemical warfare drove soldiers out of the trenches and into battle.

CHEMICAL WARFARE

The trenches of World War I were meant to be a temporary solution, giving men shelter as they held their positions. When artillery proved incapable of forcing either side out of these earthworks, various innovators set to work finding other ways to force out trench-bound men and get the war moving. The solution came from scientific laboratories and earned the war one of its nicknames, the Chemists' War.

CHLORINE GAS

Before the Germans used chlorine gas at Ypres, they had tried using xylyl-bromide, a type of tear gas, on the eastern front. On January 31, 1915, in Bolimow, Russia, the Germans fired shells loaded with liquid tear gas, but the liquid didn't disperse through

TEAR GAS GRENADES

When the French government drafted policemen to fight as soldiers in the war, the men brought their police weapons with them into the trenches. One of the weapons they brought was a rifle grenade, or rifle shell, that contained tear gas. Unlike the xyxyl-bromide used by Germans, these cartridges used ethyl-bromacetate gas. Both chemicals acted as eye and skin irritants and had been used by the French for several years to disperse civilian riots. Tear gas was the first chemical weapon used in the war.

the cold air. Because the temperatures were well below zero degrees Fahrenheit (-18°C), the liquid simply froze and fell to the ground.

Scientist Fritz Haber was working to develop a chemical weapon for the Germans. The liquid tear gas failure at Bolimow convinced him he needed to find a chemical that would be gaseous and not liquid at normal temperatures. After considering a variety of chemicals, Haber selected chlorine. Not only was chlorine gaseous until well below zero degrees Fahrenheit, but it was also two and a half times heavier than air. With this weight, chlorine gas would roll across the landscape, fill holes and trenches, and resist being scattered by the wind.

Haber didn't want to deliver chlorine in artillery shells because he calculated it would take 72,000 artillery shells to get enough chemical into the air to affect the enemy. Instead, he planned to transport the gas in cylinders similar to scuba tanks. In using cylinders, deploying the gas would then simply be a matter of placing the cylinders and opening the valves when the wind was blowing in the right direction.

Despite reluctance from the German military to accept Haber's new weapon, Haber convinced an army captain to allow one company to be trained in the use of chlorine gas as a weapon. By mid-February of 1915, 6,000 canisters of chlorine gas were in place in the German trenches at Ypres. Haber chose this location because the wind tended to blow from the German trenches toward the Allied trenches. But for two full months after the cylinders were in place, the wind blew in the wrong direction. By March 25, Haber had moved the cylinders to utilize this new wind pattern and was once again ready to test his new weapon.

When released, the gas rolled across the landscape and quickly incapacitated the Allied soldiers, opening up a four-mile

Haber experimenting in his lab

FRITZ HABER

1868–1934

Fritz Haber was born into a wealthy German-Jewish family and studied at several universities. In 1891, he earned a doctorate degree in organic chemistry. He later worked in physical chemistry, focusing on industrial or other large-scale applications for various chemical processes.

Following the war, he received the Nobel Prize for Chemistry in 1918 for perfecting a process of ammonia synthesis. During the war, the British navy blockaded Germany and cut off the nation's supply of nitrates from Chile. Without nitrates, Germany couldn't manufacture wartime explosives or fertilizer to grow crops. Haber's process created the ammonia used to create nitrates and allowed Germany to remain in the war despite the blockade.

After World War I, Haber continued to work as the head of the Kaiser Wilhelm Institute for Physical Chemistry and Electrochemistry, a position he had held since 1911. In 1933, the Nazi Party's race laws called for the resignation of his largely Jewish staff. Haber resigned along with his fellow Jewish scientists and went into exile in England. He spent four months working at the University of Cambridge but worried the cold winters in England were harmful to his health. He moved to Basel, Switzerland, but only lived there for a few months before dying of a massive heart attack.

(6 km) gap in the Allied defenses. Unfortunately, the German troops were unable to permanently hold the Allied trenches. In terms of territory, Haber's success was only temporary, but the paranoia and the panic it caused were permanent.

BRITISH BLUNDERS

As soon as scientists in the United Kingdom realized chlorine had been used against their soldiers, they began working on their own chlorine gas. General Douglas Haig ordered the delivery of 5,000 150-pound (68 kg) chlorine-filled cylinders to the front lines for use at the battle of Loos in 1915.[1]

Because the gas couldn't simply be unloaded from a truck at the front trench, each of the 5,000 cylinders had to be carried through the communications trenches on the shoulders of two men. In addition to the men carrying the gas itself, other soldiers carried awkward lengths of pipe to spray the gas out of the trench and into no-man's-land. Rain fell throughout

GIVING IT A SHOT

In addition to figuring out how to make chlorine gas work in battle, Haber also contended with the conservative German military. Military campaigns had traditionally relied on artillery to break into a fortified area and force out the enemy. Chemicals were previously untested in battle and, to many of the military men, they were considered less honorable. These men also doubted how effective the chlorine gas would be. But artillery wasn't working, and the longer both sides remained entrenched, the harder it became to get the necessary artillery even as the officers watched their men's morale sink lower and lower. Because they needed to try something new, they agreed to let Haber have his battle, but they didn't expect success.

the delivery, and the men had to slog through 3.5 miles (5.6 km) of trenches that in some places were one foot (0.3 m) deep in water. It took between seven and eight hours to get everything in place.

On the morning of September 25, there was only a very slight breeze. Instead of waiting for better conditions as the Germans had done, Haig ordered the gas released on schedule. In other areas, the gas simply lingered in no-man's-land, where British soldiers struggling through up to ten rows of barbed wire to reach the German trenches encountered it. Some of the gas actually drifted back into the Allied trenches, and by the time the day ended, British forces had suffered more casualties from their own gas than had

General Haig helped bring chemical warfare into the Allied arsenal.

the Germans. All in all, it was a much less successful attack than the German attack at Ypres.

THE KING OF GASES

Chlorine and tear gas weren't the only gases used in the trenches. The French developed phosgene, which combined chlorine with carbon monoxide to create a product ten times as deadly as chlorine alone. Similar to chlorine, phosgene is heavier than air and stays close to the ground, where it settles in depressions such as trenches and craters. The effects are similar to those of chlorine gas, but because there is less coughing caused by this gas, men were less likely to realize they were being exposed and put on gas masks.

The Germans also developed several gases that could penetrate the gas masks used by soldiers and then cause nausea. The soldier would then remove his mask to vomit and be exposed to other gases already released in the environment.

ENEMY DEAD

It was impossible to tell how many dead enemy soldiers lay in the terrain between trenches. But with so little territory changing hands, the number of enemies dead was the new standard by which success was measured. The United Kingdom's General Douglas Haig no longer sought to break through the German trenches but instead focused on a "wearing out fight."[2] He often had no real estimates of enemy casualties, and he assumed German losses corresponded closely to losses among his own forces. Because of this, Haig sometimes flew into a rage when he didn't think his own troops had lost enough men, fearing German losses had also been too low.

By far the most deadly of the chemical weapons sent into the trenches was mustard gas, which came to be known as the king of gases. Mustard gas was named for its faint sulfur smell and for the yellow blisters it formed when it came into contact with a soldier's skin. A very small amount of mustard gas was added to an explosive shell. When this shell detonated, the thick, oily liquid became a dangerous mist. Gas masks only did so much to protect against mustard gas because the gas penetrated clothing and leather, leaving oozing yellow blisters wherever it touched. If it got into a soldier's eyes, he would soon be unable to see as his eyes oozed and crusted over. A man who breathed it in would find himself rasping for breath around the blisters in his throat and lungs. In mild cases, men could fully recover, but extended exposure led to permanent scars and blindness.

URINE MASKS

Before the Germans used chlorine gas at Ypres, they requisitioned 20,000 gas masks for their own men.[3] The soldiers of the United Kingdom weren't so lucky; they didn't have masks and had to make do with whatever was handy. Chlorine breaks down in water, and the immediate solution was for the men to use gauze, or even an extra sock, and urinate on it and then tie this makeshift mess to their faces.

Soldiers exposed to mustard gas had to bathe with hot water and soap within 30 minutes of exposure to avoid blistering. This required portable shower units with specially trained medics who also made certain the men's eyes were washed and collected their contaminated uniforms for cleaning. A single gassed soldier could spread the oily film from himself and thus contaminate the ambulance, the medical staff, and fellow patients.

One of the scariest effects of mustard gas was that it was very slow acting. Because the oily chemical did not break down in water, an area bombed with mustard gas was a potential danger long after the gas was no longer visible. The chemical settled into ditches and even in innocent-looking puddles, where it could be stirred up again if the soil or water were disturbed by man or animal.

In three weeks of mustard gas shelling at Ypres, the forces from the United Kingdom had more than 14,000 men wounded or killed.[4] The point of using a chemical agent, such as chlorine gas or even mustard gas, wasn't necessarily to kill as many soldiers as possible. Taking a man out of the fight even temporarily was just as good, and the longer he remained useless as a soldier, the better. It took men on average 45 days to recover from phosgene exposure, 46 days to recover from mustard gas exposure, and 60 days to recover from chlorine gas exposure.

Soldiers fighting on the eastern front faced terrain marked by mountains and cold temperatures.

CHAPTER
8

TRENCHES OUTSIDE THE WESTERN FRONT

Trench warfare wasn't confined to the western front. It also took place in the Ottoman Empire, in Italy, and on the eastern front. Because the local terrain and circumstances of the war varied from place to place, no two fronts were identical.

RUSSIAN TRENCHES

The eastern front was 1,000 miles (1,600 km) long and lacked the amount of soldiers seen in the west. Still, Russia threw men into battle, losing two entire armies, or 250,000 men, in 1914 alone.[1] These were the battles that sent German soldiers toward the eastern front, compromised the Schlieffen Plan, and sent the western front into the trenches.

With armies stretched across vast distances, the eastern trenches were never as extensive or as permanent as those on the western front. Similar to the trenches on the western front, eastern trenches zigzagged across the landscape. They were almost five feet (1.5 m) deep with dugouts extending from the sides. In areas where the groundwater was near the surface, a dugout might be less than two feet (0.6 m) tall, but ideally, they were as deep as the trench itself. The roof of a Russian dugout was made from whatever materials the men found readily available, such as straw, sticks, or scrap metal from a downed aircraft, all covered with dirt. In the summer, the dugout door might be a man's cape, but in the winter, they would use the more weather-resistant lid of an ammo box. A dugout near the rear, used by officers, had a roof of several layers of logs and earth to better protect the officers inside from the direct impact of an artillery shell.

The dugouts and trenches provided shelter from enemy soldiers and artillery and also sheltered the men from the weather. Russian dugouts contained small stoves as well as insulated bottles of tea and porridge. The cold along the eastern front was what had made German tear gas unusable at the battle of Bolimov when the chemical froze and dropped uselessly to the ground. In these icy conditions, soldiers on both sides suffered from cold-related problems, such as frostbite. Although the Russians had fewer of these weather issues than the Germans, the Russian and Romanian soldiers, both fighting for the Allies, welcomed the care and assistance of nurses from the United Kingdom.

ITALIAN TRENCHES

The Italian trenches took the battle between Italy and Austria-Hungary to the high altitudes of the Alps, a European mountain range that crosses into eight countries including France, Italy, and Switzerland. This meant parts of the Italian front lay at altitudes exceeding 6,500 feet (2,000 m). Yet again, entirely new systems of war needed to be developed, in part because of the terrain. Mountain slopes rose at steep angles approaching 80 degrees, and because of this, rivers ran fast through glacial valleys. This meant there were almost no roads or railroads in the area, so both militaries built roads and erected bridges wherever they could. Where this was impossible, the Italians used cable cars and mules to transport food and munitions to battle sites high in the mountains.

GRAY PARTRIDGES

Doctors and nurses of the Scottish women's ambulance corps contacted the War Office in London and volunteered their services for the duration of World War I. When their own government told them to keep quiet and stay home, the women approached other Allied governments and were encouraged by the French to serve in Romania. To reach this area, they sailed across the Baltic Sea and traveled across Russia, where they reported to the Russian General Staff for duty. The Romanian soldiers welcomed them and called them Gray Partridges because of their gray uniforms.

Once the soldiers got into place, they needed protection not only from the enemy but from the bitter weather, because at these altitudes, low temperatures averaged 23 degrees Fahrenheit (-5°C). The men dug trenches through the snow and ice and used explosives to shatter mountain rock to create caves and tunnels.

Working and fighting at these altitudes took special training. Soldiers in both the Austrian and Italian armies learned to move on skis and work with ice picks, wearing snowsuits and goggles when traversing the glaciers. To cross these ice sheets, both armies needed local guides and recruited men from nearby villages. Because of this, families often had men fighting on both sides of the war, and stories exist of a soldier in the heat of battle hearing a cousin or brother's voice coming from among the enemy.

Despite the precautions taken and the shelter of trench and tunnel, death came most often not from battle itself but from the weather. Men, especially the wounded who might not be mobile, suffered from frostbite. In addition, thousands of men

FROSTBITE

Frostbite, or the freezing of skin and muscle, can happen in less than 30 minutes when a person's skin is exposed to extremely cold air. At first, the skin turns pink, then tingles, and then hurts, and the person shivers. A person with extreme frostbite will get sleepy and confused as the frostbitten skin goes numb, freezes, and dies and the person's body temperature drops. To prevent frostbite, soldiers had to keep skin covered and warm and limit their exposure to wind and cold. Mildly frostbitten skin and muscle needed to be warmed gradually. In extreme cases, doctors amputated the dead tissue, often fingers or toes.

Members of the Russian military construct a railway track in March 1916.

died in avalanches when snow and ice would sheet off the side of the mountain, destroying everything in the avalanche's path as it roared downhill.

Known as Ski Brigades, German soldiers learned to fight in ski equipment and snowsuits.

TURKISH TRENCHES

As nation sided against nation, the Ottoman Empire joined the Central powers of Germany and Austria-Hungary in late 1914. This meant control of the Ottoman

sea passage to Russia, known as the
Dardanelles, was controlled by the Central
powers. The United Kingdom needed to
get help to the Russians, who were still
fighting the Germans on the eastern front.
The British decided to use its navy to
knock the Ottoman Empire out of the war.
It could then aid the Russians and draw
German troops away from the western
front to break the war out of the trenches.
The naval assault began in February 1915,
but the land-based Ottoman forts fired
back at the ships and also laid mines and
floating bombs in the shipping channels.

ICEMEN

Melting mountain glaciers in the Italian Alps
have revealed the bodies of men who fought in
the Italian trenches. Buried in the ice, they were
preserved so well that those who found them
could tell which ones were blond, blue-eyed
Austrians. Three men who were found hanging
out of a wall of ice had rolls of bandages in their
pockets, which indicated to researchers they
were probably stretcher bearers. Because many
local men fought on both sides of the conflict,
the unnamed soldiers have been buried in the
village cemetery.

Because their naval assault failed, the French and British decided to use
ground troops. On April 25, 1915, the Allies attacked on land in an area known
as Gallipoli. The British military's Australian and New Zealand Army Corps
soldiers, known as the ANZACs, stormed the beach. As Turkish reinforcements
arrived, the ANZAC soldiers were forced back, where they dug small shelter
holes to get below ground and out of reach of the artillery. They joined these
individual holes to form trenches, creating the position the Allies held with very

The British ship HMS *Cornwallis* fires at the Turkish troops at Gallipoli.

little change for the next eight months. These ANZAC trenches looked similar to the trenches dug by other Allied forces on the western front. However, the soldiers from the Ottoman Empire didn't dig interconnected trenches in rows of three. Their trenches formed labyrinth-like patterns that sprawled across the landscape.

The Gallipoli no-man's-land was, at its widest, only 30 feet (9 m) across. In other places, the Turkish trenches were on one side of a ridge with the ANZAC trenches on the other and nothing but a strand of barbed wire in between. In these areas, the men were close enough to hear each other's conversations, and in one area in particular, the Allies could smell the bread baking in the Turkish ovens.

Because no-man's-land was so narrow, the soldiers did not patrol or dig new trenches under the cover of darkness. Instead, new trenches were constructed underground with the soldiers digging out a forward tunnel and, only at the last moment, opening the roof to create a new trench. Instead of forming new trenches, sometimes these tunnels were used as potential traps with their thin roofs left in place so they looked like solid ground an enemy force could safely cross, but would actually collapse under the weight of advancing troops, dropping them into holes several feet deep.

In addition to the shallow tunnels that could become trenches or traps, both sides dug much deeper tunnels. These deeper ANZAC diggings created a complex

array of tunnels and galleries facing the Turkish tunnels. ANZAC soldiers took up listening posts in these caverns so they could detect any Turkish attempts to tunnel toward the ANZAC line.

After remaining in place for almost eight months, the Allies initiated a secret evacuation that took place in several stages from December 1915 to January 1916. As the majority of ANZAC soldiers marched to the beaches where they would board ships, the remaining group of soldiers attacked the Turks with infantry, mines, and hand grenades to create a distraction. Because huge numbers of casualties were predicted but very few occurred, some historians consider this the most successful part of the entire campaign for the Allies because its

British troops take shelter underground at Gallipoli.

ANZAC TRENCHES

Of all the trenches dug in World War I, those of the Ottoman Empire, now modern Turkey, are the best preserved because they were not dug in snow or in agricultural fields. Because erosion will wipe them out in the next 50 years, a team of archaeologists began investigating them in 2010. The field crew from New Zealand had to learn to tell the difference between an eroded trench and a collapsed tunnel. They discovered that even when walls collapse as the walls crumble and soil slides back into a trench, these partially filled trenches still zigzag and have flat floors.

Tunnels ran long and straight and tended to collapse, leaving an uneven surface. The group also found a variety of ammunition ranging from enormous warship shells to bullets labeled in Arabic, as well as food containers, flagons for liquor, canteens, and buttons. They discovered many more items left by the ANZAC forces than by Turkish soldiers, most likely because the ANZAC soldiers pulled out quickly and quietly, leaving the Turkish forces to make a more leisurely exit.

results were better than planned. Of the combined total of one million soldiers who fought at Gallipoli, approximately 333,000 were casualties, with up to 130,000 dead.[2]

Communists took control of Russia in the spring of 1917, eventually leading to new leadership pulling Russia out of the war.

CHAPTER
★ 9 ★

LEAVING THE TRENCHES

As the war in the trenches dragged on, the various governments involved grew desperate. With the armies remaining in place in the trenches, they used masses of ammunition and sacrificed men's lives to no avail. It was time to move the war back out into open countryside.

After communists seized control in Russia, they pulled that country out of the war on March 3, 1918. With the end of fighting on the eastern front, German soldiers who had been fighting there, as well as those who had been Russian prisoners of war, would be freed for other duty. This meant Germany would be able to transfer thousands of men to the western front and get the war moving

RED RUSSIANS

Nine years before entering World War I, Russia had lost a war against Japan. When the Russian army took heavy losses early in World War I, the people blamed the czar, Russia's hereditary ruler. As the protests mounted, he stepped down, leaving two groups vying for power: the conservative White Russians, and the Bolsheviks, known as Reds. When the Bolsheviks, who became known as communists, eventually took control of Russia, their leaders pulled Russia out of the war.

again. The Germans wanted to accomplish this before the United States—which had declared war in 1917 and had relatively few troops in Europe until 1918—was fully committed to the war.

Before entering the war, the United States had long been isolationist, leaving other countries to solve their own problems. It was hard to get people to support a war in part because of the many European soldiers losing their lives. No one wanted to send that many US soldiers to their deaths if war could be avoided. Eventually, the sinking of US ships by German U-boats and German plans to encourage a Mexican invasion of the United States convinced people war was inevitable, although it would take time to draft and train an army large enough to send abroad.

The Germans predicted the United States would send large numbers of men, and they were right. By 1918, US troops were leaving for France at the rate of 10,000 men a day.[1] Before US troop commitments could reach this point, the Germans launched a plan that looked deceptively like a retreat.

US soldiers say good-bye to their sweethearts before heading to war in 1917.

GERMAN RETREAT

In February 1917, German soldiers pulled out of the trenches, but they hadn't given up. This was the opening move in Operation Alberich. The Germans knew the Allies were massing for a major offensive, and they knew their own line had weak points where a well-planned Allied attack might break through. Instead of trying to reinforce these problem areas, they built a new and improved defensive line farther back, called the Hindenburg Line. As the Germans withdrew to this new point, they destroyed everything in their path. They burned crops and anything the Allies could use for food, destroyed bridges, burned homes, and also set a wide range of traps.

Although the Allies took some ground, casualty counts were massive. At Vimy Ridge, the Canadians sent 100,000 men into battle with 11,000 casualties, including nearly 3,600 killed.[2] In ten days of fighting at Chemin des Dames, the French lost 30,000 men.[3] The Germans hadn't simply retreated—they were still ready to fight.

The military leaders from the United Kingdom wanted out of the trenches just as badly as the Germans did. If they couldn't blast the Germans out with artillery, they would do it from below with mines. Moving north of the new trench line to an area near Ypres, the British brought in moles, shovels, and mines for the battles of Messines. The resulting explosion was so huge it could be heard as far away as London. It was time to drive the Germans out of their trenches once and for all.

TANKS

Tanks were not the first armored land vehicles used in World War I. Armored cars had been popular early in the war before the trenches were dug. The tank differed from many other military vehicles in that it had segmented caterpillar tracks, similar to those on the tractors used by US farmers, instead of wheels.

Tank tracks functioned well because they could easily handle mud and uneven terrain, both of which could bog down the wheels of a car or truck.

The United Kingdom already used caterpillar tractors in France to haul heavy guns from place to place.

By June 1915, a plan was in place for a new vehicle that would be able to reach speeds of seven miles per hour (11 kmh) on flat land, turn sharply at this top rate of speed, climb a five-foot (1.5 m) earth wall, such as a trench wall, cross an eight-foot (2.4 m) gap, greater than the width of most trenches, and fire from both machine guns and small cannons. As the United Kingdom developed these vehicles, Winston Churchill, the United Kingdom's First Lord of the Admiralty, called them land ships. To keep the plans a secret, they were code-named tanks, referring to water tanks, and it was this name that eventually stuck.

Tanks did not have an encouraging beginning; two days after the first test tank rolled off the production line, its tracks came off. Just over a week later, it happened again. On January 29, 1916, the first completed tank, known as Big Willie, was demonstrated for various officials in the United Kingdom. It performed so well that by February 12, the Ministry of Munitions ordered 100 tanks. Once the tanks were built, the military had to find men to operate them, but this proved problematic. Very few people had experience with mechanical vehicles of any kind. The people they could find who had mechanical experience had no experience with the military or in battle. This meant training would take time.

Between building tanks and recruiting men, it was hard to get everything and everyone coordinated. Sometimes a crew was pulled together only to realize they had no tank because their designated vehicle had already suffered a breakdown. Because crews had to share tanks for training, they had very little practice. Many had no practice following orders or reading a map or compass.

Given these training limitations and the small number of tanks, it is no surprise the tanks and their crews performed poorly at the battle of the Somme on September 15, 1916. By the time the tanks were used again at Cambrai in November 20, 1917, the United Kingdom had amassed 381 crewed vehicles, and because of this, they were able to show the Germans just what a fleet of tanks could do.[4] They breached 12 miles (19 km) of the German front, capturing 10,000 prisoners, 123 guns, and 281 machine guns.[5] In fact, they advanced so quickly the infantry was unable to keep up.

STORMTROOPERS

As the militaries worked to drive each other out of the trenches, they developed fast-moving shock troops. Perhaps the most well-known were the German stormtroopers. On March 21, 1918, the Germans attacked the Allied line, opening with a creeping barrage, a battlefield tactic they had learned from the United Kingdom. To create the barrage, gunners fired a curtain of artillery shells, sending out clouds of smoke and poisonous gas. As men put on their gas masks—or took them off to vomit depending on the type of gas—a party of

TANK TROUBLES

When the United Kingdom launched its tanks at the Somme, the Germans were remarkably unimpressed with these huge vehicles. Each measured 32 feet (10 m) long, weighed 28 short tons (25 metric tons), and moved at a top speed of four miles (6 km) per hour. In some models, the radiator, which cooled the engine, was located in the crew cabin, causing the interior of the tank to heat up to 125 degrees Fahrenheit (52°C). The men operating the tanks often passed out from the heat combined with the engine fumes. Of the 49 tanks that made their debut at the Somme, all but 18 broke down or got stuck, and because they moved so slowly, they also made easy artillery targets.[6]

German stormtroopers use a flamethrower in a trench attack in 1917.

stormtroopers charged out of the gas clouds and leapt into the British trenches. Each stormtrooper was armed with a rifle, but his weapon of choice was the hand grenade, which stormtroopers carried bags of into battle. Some men carried flamethrowers, mortars, machine pistols, or sawed-off artillery pieces, ready to create devastation in the trenches. If they came upon a heavily defended area, they simply passed around it and moved on to another area they could easily take. This didn't happen often because they generally outnumbered the force they were attacking three to one. In less than a day, German stormtroopers took the Allied front line and pushed into open country, opening gaps along a 40-mile (60 km) section of the western front.

The trenches had provided relative safety for the battling troops for approximately two years, but mines, poisonous gases, tanks, and specially trained troops meant these earthworks were no longer the barriers they had been early in the war. They could be driven over or blown up and provide a cavity to trap poison capable of killing men for weeks. The days of fighting in the trenches had finally passed. Before the war ended, approximately 8,500,000 men would be killed and another 21,200,000 wounded.[7]

The men who returned home seldom discussed what they had experienced in the trenches. Instead, they tried to forget the sights, smells, and horrors. In Europe, the trenches disappeared as the land was plowed for crops. As global temperatures rise, receding Italian glaciers reveal soldiers' burials, bringing the fates of some soldiers to light. Still more is being learned as historians and archaeologists explore Turkish trenches before they too crumble away and are gone.

A BROTHERHOOD

Men who served in the trenches of World War I experienced things that could be understood only by other trench veterans. Because of this, many of the men simply kept quiet about what they had seen and done, although some of these men wrote about their experiences in their journals. The British National Archives is working to make the journals in its collection available online so researchers and students will have access to a more complete picture of World War I.

TIMELINE

October 6, 1908

Austria-Hungary annexes Bosnia-Herzegovina.

June 28, 1914

A member of the Black Hand military group assassinates Archduke Franz Ferdinand.

July 28, 1914

Austria-Hungary declares war on Serbia.

August 4, 1914

Germany invades Belgium.

September 25, 1915

At the battle of Loos, General Haig orders the use of chlorine gas.

December 1915–January 1916

ANZAC forces pull out of Gallipoli.

September 15, 1916

Tanks from the United Kingdom debut at the battle of the Somme.

February 1917

Germans initiate Operation Alberich.

December 25, 1914

Soldiers take part in the Christmas Truce.

January 31, 1915

At Bolimow, Russia, the Germans attack with tear gas but, because of the cold, it fails to disperse.

April 22, 1915

At the battle of Ypres, Germans successfully attack the Allies with chlorine gas.

April 25, 1915

ANZAC forces invade Gallipoli.

June 7, 1917

In the battle of Messines, the Allies use mines to kill approximately 10,000 men.

November 20, 1917

British tanks devastate the German line.

March 3, 1918

Russians sign a treaty with the Central powers and pull out of the war.

March 21, 1918

German Stormtroopers attack and break the Allied line.

ESSENTIAL FACTS

KEY PLAYERS

- General Alexander von Kluck was blamed for the failure of the Schlieffen Plan because he chose an alternate path for his men, leaving a gap in the German defense.

- Chemist Fritz Haber developed a variety of chemical processes and weapons, including chlorine gas, that benefitted the Germans throughout the war.

- John Norton-Griffiths trained the British miners who dug the tunnels and laid the mines beneath the German trenches at the battle of Messines.

KEY EVENTS

- When the Germans failed to quickly take Belgium and France using the Schlieffen Plan, they fell back to a line of trenches that sheltered their soldiers from Allied artillery.

- Trench warfare was unlike conventional war, and soldiers needed to be retrained to not look over the trench wall, to fight in close quarters, and to always keep their feet dry to avoid trench foot, all while artillery shells pounded down, churning up the earth.

- Several inventions made staying in the trenches less desirable—chlorine and mustard gases both collected in the trenches, turning them into poisonous pits. With the addition of the tank, mines, and anti-trench troops, trench warfare came to an end.

IMPACT ON SOCIETY

Without the trenches, World War I might have been over much faster. These earthworks provided protection for the soldiers, but also led to numerous scientific innovations, including chemical weapons, some of which are still used against people today.

QUOTE

"No-man's-land under snow is like the face of the moon: chaotic, crater ridden, uninhabitable, awful, the abode of madness."

—*Wilfred Owen, a soldier and poet from the United Kingdom*

GLOSSARY

ARTILLERY
Large guns manned by a crew of operators used to shoot long distances.

CASUALTY
A person killed or injured during a war.

CHLORINE GAS
A chemical that is a gas at normal temperatures and, when inhaled, blisters the lungs.

DUCKBOARD
A platform or board made from wooden slats. The gaps allow water to drain through.

FIRE STEP
A ledge on which soldiers stand and fire out of a trench at the enemy.

INFANTRY
Soldiers who fight on foot; the branch of the army including these soldiers.

LATRINE
A toilet, especially one used in a military setting.

NO-MAN'S-LAND
The dangerous territory lying between opposing trenches targeted by artillery and snipers and lined with barbed wire obstructions to slow enemy advances.

PILLBOX
A small concrete structure for machine guns or other weapons.

SHRAPNEL
Shell fragments from an exploded shell.

SNIPER
An infantry rifleman whose task is to kill individual enemy soldiers at long range.

TEAR GAS
A variety of nerve gases that act against the body's pain sensors. People who are gassed cry, cough, and vomit.

TRENCH FOOT
A fungal infection soldiers often developed when standing in water for long periods.

ADDITIONAL RESOURCES

SELECTED BIBLIOGRAPHY

Gilbert, Martin. *The Somme: Heroism and Horror in the First World War.* New York: Holt, 2006. Print.

Hochschild, Adam. *To End All Wars: A Story of Loyalty and Rebellion, 1914-1918.* Boston, MA: Houghton Mifflin, 2012. Print.

FURTHER READINGS

Duffy, Chris, ed. *Above the Dreamless Dead: World War I in Poetry and Comics.* New York: First Second, 2014. Print.

Grant, R.G. *World War I: The Definitive Visual History: From Sarajevo to Versailles.* New York: DK, 2014. Print.

Hale, Nathan. *Treaties, Trenches, Mud, and Blood.* New York: Amulet, 2014. Print.

WEBSITES

To learn more about Essential Library of World War I, visit **booklinks.abdopublishing.com**. These links are routinely monitored and updated to provide the most current information available.

PLACES TO VISIT

Imperial War Museum London
Lambeth Road
London SE1 6HZ, UK
44 (0) 20 7416 5000
http://www.iwm.org.uk/visits/iwm-london
An extensive museum with multiple locations, the London location has new First World War galleries. The exhibits cover life at home as well as what was happening at the front.

The National World War I Museum and Memorial
100 West Twenty-Sixth Street
Kansas City, MO 64108
816-888-8100
https://theworldwar.org
Exhibits and educational programs explore the history of World War I and share stories through the eyes of those who lived it. The museum is attached to the Liberty Memorial, a monument to those who served.

SOURCE NOTES

CHAPTER 1. A PECULIAR FOG

1. David Roberts, ed. "Wilfred Owen: Dulce et Decorum Est." *The War Poetry Website*. The War Poetry Website, n.d. Web. 6 May 2015.

2. Robert E. Cook. "The Mist that Rolled into the Trenches: Chemical Escalation in World War I." *Bulletin of the Atomic Scientists*, Jan. 1971. 38.

CHAPTER 2. TEMPORARY TRENCHES TURNED LONG-TERM

None.

CHAPTER 3. TRENCH DESIGNS

1. Jon Stallworthy. *Wilfred Owen*. London: Oxford UP, 1974. Print. 158.

CHAPTER 4. MEDICAL MATTERS

1. Edgar Jones, et al. "Shell Shock: An Outcome Study of a First World War 'PIE' Unit." *Psychological Medicine* 37 (2007): 216–217. Print.

2. Martin Gilbert. *The Somme: Heroism and Horror in the First World War*. New York: MacMillan, 2007. Print. 194.

3. Owain Clarke. "World War One: Medical Advances Inspired by the Conflict." *BBC*. BBC, 7 Aug. 2014. Web. 5 May 2015.

4. Michael Duffy. "Body Lice." *FirstWorldWar.com*. Michael Duffy, 22 Aug. 2009. Web. 21 May 2015.

5. "Vaccine Usage in Military Medicine: The Forefront of Disease Prevention." *Milvax*. Immunization Healthcare Branch of the Defense Health Agency, n.d. Web. 14 May 2015.

CHAPTER 5. ADAPTING TO TRENCH WARFARE

1. "What Really Happened in the Christmas Truce of 1914?" *BBC*. BBC, n.d. Web. 14 May 2015.

2. Kate Ravilious. "The Great War in Miniature." *Archaeology* Sept. 2014: 35. Print.

CHAPTER 6. DAILY SCHEDULE

1. "How Did 12 Million Letters Reach WWI Soldiers Each Week?" *BBC*. BBC, n.d. Web. 14 May 2015.

CHAPTER 7. CHEMICAL WARFARE

1. Adam Hoschschild. *To End All Wars*. Boston: Houghton Mifflin Harcourt, 2011. Print. 163.

2. Ibid. 209.

3. Ibid. 142.

4. Robert E. Cook. "The Mist that Rolled into the Trenches: Chemical Escalation in World War I." *Bulletin of the Atomic Scientists*, Jan. 1971. 38.

SOURCE NOTES
CONTINUED

CHAPTER 8. TRENCHES OUTSIDE THE WESTERN FRONT

1. Jonathan Smele. "War and Revolution in Russia: 1914–1921." *BBC*. BBC, 10 Mar. 2011. Web. 28 May 2015.

2. Samir S. Patel. "Anzac's Next Chapter: Archaeologists Conduct the First-ever Survey of the Legendary WWI Battlefield at Gallipoli." *Archaeology* May 2013: 56. Print.

CHAPTER 9. LEAVING THE TRENCHES

1. Seán Lang. *First World War for Dummies*. West Sussex, UK: John Wiley and Sons, 2014. Print. 226.

2. "The Battle of Vimy Ridge." *Veteran Affairs Canada*. Veteran Affairs Canada, n.d. Web. 30 June 2015.

3. Rick Smith. "France Commemorates a Dark Chapter in World War I History." *The New York Times*. The New York Times Company, 15 Apr. 2007. Web. 30 June 2015.

4. C. N. Trueman. "Tanks and World War One." *The History Learning Site*. HistoryLearningSite.co.uk, n.d. Web. 29 May 2015.

5. Ibid.

6. Ibid.

7. "WWI Casualty and Death Tables." *PBS.org*. PBS, n.d. Web. 30 June 2015.

INDEX

Allied forces, 5, 19, 85
amputation, 35, 36, 80
Art of War, 19
Australian and New Zealand Army
    Corps, 83–87
Austria-Hungary, 5, 13–14, 79, 82

barbed wire, 30–31, 45–46, 48, 49,
    72, 85
barrage, 95
battles
    battle of Bolimov, 78
    battle of Loos, 71
    battle of the Marne, 17
    battle of Messines, 52, 53, 54,
        92
    battle of the Somme, 46, 94, 95
bayonets, 39, 49, 57
Belgium, 5, 16, 21
Black Hand, 14
Bosnia-Herzegovina, 13–14
British National Archives, 97

casualties, 10, 72, 73, 86–87, 92
Central powers, 5, 82–83
Chemin des Dames, 92
chlorine gas, 7, 8, 10–11, 67–69,
    71, 73, 74, 75
Christmas Truce of 1914, 48, 50
Churchill, Winston, 94
communication trench, 24, 26,
    30–31
communists, 89, 90

daily routine, 5, 48, 57, 58
Dardanelles, 83
draft, 62, 68, 90
dressing station, 26, 30–31, 34, 35
dugouts, 26, 30–31, 35, 48, 49, 78
"Dulce et Decorum Est," 6

eastern front, 16, 67, 77–78, 83, 89
electric shock, 35

fire step, 38, 44, 57, 60
firing line, 24, 26, 30–31
flanks, 17, 19
France, 5, 8, 10, 14, 16, 21, 27, 62,
    79, 90, 93
Franz Ferdinand, 14
frostbite, 79, 80

Gallipoli, 48, 83, 85, 87
gangrene, 36
gas cylinders, 68–69, 71
gas fright, 7
gas masks, 7, 10, 73–74, 95
Germany, 5, 8, 14, 16, 48, 70, 82,
    89
Gray Partridges, 79
grenades, 8, 49, 68, 86, 96

Haber, Fritz, 68–71
Hague Treaty, 8
Haig, Douglas, 71–72, 73
helmets, 6, 45, 58
Hindenburg Line, 91

Italy, 5, 77, 79

Jones, Robert, 38

Kluck, Alexander von, 17–19

letters, 58, 60, 62
lice, 38, 40–41

machine guns, 28, 45, 46, 49, 58,
    94, 95
mines, 52–54, 83, 86, 92, 97
mole men, 52, 92
morning hate, 58
mustard gas, 74–75

nationalism, 14
Nicholas II, 8
nighttime raids, 49
no-man's-land, 28–29, 30–31, 38,
    45, 50, 52, 58, 60, 71, 72, 85
Norton-Griffiths, John, 52–53

observation trees, 48
Operation Alberich, 91
Ottoman Empire, 5, 13, 48, 77, 82–83, 85, 87
Owen, Wilfred, 6, 29

Paris, France, 16–17, 18, 19
periscope, 44–45
phosgene, 73, 75
pillboxes, 48
post-traumatic stress disorder, 33
Princip, Gavrilo, 14

Race to the Sea, 21
rats, 38–41
reserve trench, 24, 26, 30–31, 60, 64
River Aisne, 19
Rivers, William, 35, 37
Roberts, Fred, 61
Russia, 5, 8, 14, 16, 67, 77–79, 83, 89, 90

sandbags, 26, 27, 58
Schlieffen, Alfred Graf von, 16
Schlieffen Plan, 16, 17, 18, 19, 78
Serbia, 13–14
shell shock, 34–35, 37
shrapnel, 44, 46
stormtroopers, 95–96
strategy, 16, 19, 21
support trench, 24, 26, 30–31, 60–61
Switzerland, 5, 21, 70, 79

talking cure, 35, 37
tanks, 92–95, 97
tear gas, 7–8, 67–68, 73, 78
tear gas grenades, 68
Thomas, Hugh Owen, 38
Thomas splint, 38
trench art, 64–65
trench design, 23–31
trench fever, 40
trench foot, 35–36, 38
trench signs, 24
Tzu, Sun, 19

United Kingdom, 5, 8, 10, 14, 21, 29, 53, 58, 61, 62, 71, 73, 74, 75, 79, 83, 92–95
United States, 5, 90

vaccines, 40
Vimy Ridge, 27, 92

western front, 5, 17, 21, 48, 50, 53, 62, 77–78, 83, 85, 89, 97
Wipers Times, the, 61
Withers, Cecil, 38
World War II, 45

xylyl-bromide, 67

Ypres, Belgium, 5, 6, 7, 8, 10, 27, 29, 34–35, 61, 67, 69, 73, 74, 75, 92

ABOUT THE AUTHOR

Sue Bradford Edwards writes nonfiction for children and teens, working from her home in Saint Louis, Missouri. She loved visiting old forts, mound sites, and ancient villages with her parents and studied archaeology and history in college. Her writing covers a range of topics including history and science.